Already There

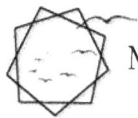

Mercury HeartLink

Already There

poems

Shirley Balance Blackwell

Already There: poems
Copyright ©2011 Shirley Balance Blackwell

ISBN: 978-0-9839935-3-7
Publisher: Mercury HeartLink
Printed in the United States of America

Front cover painting: Study At a Reading Desk (1877)
by Lord Frederick Leighton(1830-1896)
Back cover photo by Louis Blackwell

Book design by Mercury HeartLink
www.heartlink.com, editor@heartlink.com

Mercury HeartLink

ACKNOWLEDGMENTS

My sincere gratitude to the following publications, in which some of these poems first appeared, often in earlier incarnations and under different titles:

Delmarva Quarterly: "If Winter Comes" (as "Trust") and "Cranes at Twilight, Dancing"
Valley Visions–Writings and Art from the Rio Abajo: "Windows of the Soul" (as "Sonnet for Wisdom"), "Here, Where Legends Tread" (as "Pulses of Tomé"), "Wrestling Match"
Central Avenue: "Rough Landing" (as "Hard Landing")
The Rag: "Frau Einstein Pours Tea," "Hoover Soul Searcher EZ-3," "Cumulo-Coquette" (as "Clouds Are Consummate Flirts"), "Moon of the Huntress" (as "Snow Moon")
Rio Rhymes and Rhythms, Valencia County News-Bulletin: "Ichthyology" (as "Fishing")

Many thanks, also, to the following anthologies in which my poems have been included:

small canyons 2 (SW Region of the Haiku Society of America): "spiral galaxies"
Along the Rio Grande–Poetry from New Mexico: "A Fishy Story," "Valley of Fires, with Snow"
Golden Words–Senior Poet Laureate Award Winners for 2010: "Sabbatical"
Adobe Walls–an anthology of New Mexico poetry, #1: "Tomorrow's Ashes, Next Year's Rain"
Adobe Walls #2: "Upon Reflection" (as "Reflection")
Adobe Walls #3: "Hole in the Night"
Fixed and Free Poetry Anthology 2011: "Low-tide Catechism"
Encore–NFSPS Prize Poems 2010: "Pantomime in Porcelain"

I am deeply indebted to four poets who showed me the way:

Dr. Gregory Candela, University of New Mexico Professor Emeritus and dear friend, in whose kitchen I learned a lesson more valuable even than those acquired in his classroom, i.e., just how much I still had to learn.

K.K. (Kitty) Todorovich, best friend and militant muse, who insisted I was already a poet and made me believe it, too–even during our master's class, when I was reduced to tears trying to understand that damned "language" poem!

Marjorie Rommel, long-distance mentor, instant friend, who "heard the clip-clapper of this tongue of wood and knew what [I] wished to sing." An astonishing woman, treasury of poetic knowledge, who has the uncanny ability to find the gold amid the dross for all those lucky enough to have her tutelage.

My grandfather, Henry Samuel Hoefflin, poet and circuit rider/preacher in the Oklahoma Territory, who died three months before I was born. I never beheld his face, but I saw his heart in the poems he left behind. Knowing your roots can drive your destiny.

P.S. Heartfelt thanks to Stewart Warren at Mercury HeartLink, publisher, coach, and creative mind. No one should enter a book writing venture alone, and I am immensely grateful for his companionship on this journey.

Contents

SCALES, FINS, FEATHERS, WINGS

TAKING FLIGHT

MAKING IT WORK

A WOMAN'S WORK

CROSSING BOUNDARIES

JUDGING BY HER WORDS

INTRODUCTION

The legend is told of Nikola Tesla, the great Serbian scientist, inventor, and occasional poet, that the concepts for his many inventions sprang into his mind fully developed and precise in every detail. What is more, these ideas or intuitive leaps were often triggered by his hearing a random word that, somewhere in the depths of his genius, held special associations for him.

Unlike Tesla's, my ideas require a lot more nurturing before they are whole. Nonetheless, I sometimes hear a phrase or see a vignette and know instantly that I have just found a poem. The idea of "finding" a poem implies that it is already there, just waiting to be discovered. Might this mean that all poems coexist?

After all, some philosophers claim that, in the context of eternity, all *moments* coexist. A proof of sorts supports this idea; the French mathematician Fourier took what most of us think of as *time* and graphed it as a wave or frequency that, theoretically, could extend to infinity. I strive to do something similar: sample a moment, graph it as a poem, and hope that it will become timeless. I don't know if most of these poems were *Already There*, but I am thankful they are *here now* to share with you.

Shirley Balance Blackwell
September 2011

DEDICATION

This book is dedicated to Louis, my husband and heart's companion. In this, as in all else in our life together, my darling, you have been my springboard to the heights and my soft place to fall.

It is also for our children, Rebecca and Kenneth, and their mates, Glen and Melanie, whom I love as my own. Thank you for your encouragement as I moved into the new role of artist. This book is for you, your children, and theirs, so they will know that poetry runs in the family and age is just another door to be opened.

Landscape, Seascape, Escape

Here, Where Legends Tread

In this sacred place, this desert mound,
flows the life force, lifeblood of this land,
pounds in magma artery, throbs through lava vein.
Old power still abides, new power is found.
Spirit echoes of both beast and man,
past and present, on this hill resound.

We hear the tread of legends in our bones,
the hoofbeat thunder massed upon the plains,
the spirit song that sped the warrior's lance
and, in a shaman's ring of glassy stones,
the   *slap-step-slap*   of feet in circled dance
on ground packed hard by sunlit, fleeting rains.

Now hear the ancient dancer's hardened heel
stamp-stamp the heartbeat rhythms of this place,
and   *clap-brush-clap*   of hands reverberate
up from the bedrock of the human race.
Like those older souls, we walk the Wheel;
our journey carves the path to sacred space.

To the sky our prayer-wreathed hands ascend,
while our feet we root in fertile earth.
We resonate with mysteries deep and old,
keep time with timeless drum heard since our birth.
On holy ground we find the blessed whole,
and chant our songs to pulses of the land.

Here, on this hill, where beast and man have trod,
harmonic to the world, we dance toward God.

Eye of the Beholder

On horizon-holding wingspan
a red-tailed hawk spirals high,
wheels above the desert marsh and sand.
With minute tilt of russet-banded tail,
she changes forward motion,
spreads feathered fingers to sail
windswept sky, earth's upper ocean.

Only one with her keen ear
can hear the stream of air
past pinions interlocked and tapered,
can hear the hum through flutelike bones,
the whispered ecstasy of those favored
few to whom this secret song is known,
the winged who sing while soaring.

Swift and stealthy high aloft,
silent as the waltz of time,
then, from her throat and sharp, hooked beak
comes a piercing, rapier shriek
to rend the calm of desert dawn
and daybreak's crystalline peace
with cry of challenge, exultation.

Through haughty yellow eye
she sees the echo of her cry
in a mouse's heart-stopped, frozen motion.
She regards its trembling, furry ear,
upward glance in fear,
and moment of still, small terror
before it scurries to its burrow.

Atop her tower of air, the hawk surveys her realm.
All stands out in clarity through her golden lens,
from distant mountains swathed in robes of plum,
crowned with clouds of winter-white ermine,
to nearby reeds that bend and sway
at river's edge, their stalks an interplay
of latticed gray and green.

If I could look with eye as piercing keen
would I focus on the beauty or the prey?

Upon Reflection

Desert dwellers, always searching for water or shady arbor,
    let their imaginations flow in liquid i
                                   m
                                      a
                                          g
                                            e,

just as we did, seeing village lights beneath a rising moon.
                 Driving into Deming from north or west or east,

===

                 we spied the town a-twinkle by 20 miles, at least,
like houseboats floating mirrored on a shimmering lagoon.

                                              e,
                                       g
                                  a
                              r
        We denied the vision was a relic of m i
preferring to pretend we sailed toward safe, familiar harbor.

CUMULO-COQUETTE

Clouds are consummate flirts
making vows they will not keep,
letting frilly petticoats peep
from beneath their skirts
of longed-for rain as they sweep
through the ballroom of the sky.

In the arms of handsome mountains,
they dance and whirl and sway,
while lonesome desert sands
hope for a glance to come their way.

Chaco Asks Questions of Its Own

A weathered canyon cuts across the dry, high desert plain,
and in its sun-cracked crevices old artifacts remain.
The ruins of native settlements a thousand years ago
still hold their secrets hidden, despite our quest to know.

Why its forty kivas? None can say for sure,
but sky-aligned geometry marks walls that still endure.
Long-lost people once supplied this trade or culture center
where monuments built, not for pride, but for the soul to enter
some other world of spirit or some universe of learning
record the course of stars, sun, moon through centuries of turning.

Our brains are fissured by our thoughts; memory carves the grooves.
The convolutions of this canyon testify to truth
that thoughts of ancient puebloans inhabit Chaco still,
sculpting scripture in the rock, cliffs, ravines, and hills.
Ideas beckon teasingly from sandstone intellect;
whispers hint at knowledge we try to resurrect.

Sentience still breathes today from walls of sun-stacked stone.
The message comes across the years, "Oh, you are not alone,
you latest ones, who think your gold and science conquers all.
What will *you* teach posterity from thousand-year-old walls?"

VALLEY OF FIRES, WITH SNOW

Along a 70-mile stretch of desolate highway that crosses the vast Tularosa Basin in
southeast New Mexico lie two unique natural wonders: Valley of Fires State Park
is a 125-square-mile field of crumpled, fissured black rock from an ancient lava
flow. A few miles away is White Sands National Monument, 275 square miles of
dazzling gypsum dunes. At the north end of these dunes is Trinity Site, where, on
16 July 1944, the first atomic bomb was tested. The aircraft Enola Gay ferried the
atomic bomb that exploded over Hiroshima, Japan, three weeks later.

From Capitan's fog-shrouded heights, the two-lane highway drops,
descends through stone-slashed mountain passes,
then arrows west across the Tularosa Basin floor

into the Valley of Fires. Miles of dark, volcanic outcrops
sprawl, now eerily quiescent, honeycombed by gases
that bubbled from the cauldron in the planet's core.

The lava flow is frozen into cinder-blackened slag.
A bighorn sheep stands sentinel on a rocky crag.

Farther down the asphalt road, along the wintry plains,
lies unholy Trinity, where, with atomic torch,
man, not nature, fused White Sands in monumental flash,

melted into shields of glass pearlescent, tiny grains.
Today, a rime of frost outlines the rugged, wind-scorched
brush, as icy mist encases ashen, struggling tufts of grass.

Black or white? No easy answers from that fateful day
that wed bright fire to silver wings of the Enola Gay.

TOMORROW'S ASHES, NEXT YEAR'S RAIN

A fire walks our blue and purple mountain.
A day ago, flames glowed in tiny streaks,
mere rivulets down ridges, fairy fountains.

Tonight, a blazing curtain drapes the peaks
while smoke ascends, as if some ancient rite
of sacrifice portends. A tendril reek

loose on the wind foretells the dreadful sight:
a growing plume of whirling sparks and cinders
spreads beneath the full moon's radiant light.

Destruction wears a dress of lunar splendor.
How can we ache with beauty amid pain,
and, in disaster, lose our hearts to wonder?

Tomorrow, ash will nourish what remains
to flourish where this blaze now sears the brain.

BOUQUET FOR THOMAS GRAY

Full many a flower is born to blush unseen,
And waste its sweetness on the desert air
–Thomas Gray, *Elegy Written in a Country Churchyard*

Full many a desert flower adorns the scene,
though Englishmen do not attend the show.
Cascades of yellow Spanish Broom will flow,
ignoring fame the poet might bestow;
Claret Cup, unsung, still crimson glows.
Full many a flower on thorn or brush is seen

by eyes that knew them long before we came.
The Wild Lantana finds an audience to share
her ruffled purple pompoms. Creatures of the air–
gleaming bees and dry-land birds drawn near
by color, nectar–daily bow to Desert Star,
the daisy lookalike ringed by rays of cream.

Scent is not wasted on the arid air.
See the hummingbird that hovers Lupine's blue,
the flush of butterflies hoping to consume
Dune Primrose promises afloat on lush perfume?
Bees nuzzling Desert Lilies quietly disprove
the lonely fate said to await the fragrant Prickly Pear.

Wildflowers do not need our elegies,
nor does their universe depend upon our seeing;
their worth is known, praise sung by lighter beings,
who taste their sweetness on the desert breeze.

GLORIA RODENTA
(Goodbye, Aunt Laverna)

The Pack Rat chose for her treasure store
a crevice 'mid rocks on the dry desert floor.
From litter and glitter grew her citadel
at the base of a *cholla*, her lone sentinel.
She dug three chambers in the heart of the midden
and gloated, "My favorite baubles are hidden!"
To keep out of sight her shiniest finds,
she wove a fence made of sharp cactus spines.

Around the full mound of rubbish and flash
she placed barbed iron wire and shards of green glass
to fend off the clever coyote or snake,
or hawk, like the Red-tailed that circled, awake
to the flicker and flurry of furry, soft ears
or long tail atremble in miserly fears.
She was quite vigilant, lived cautiously,
hoarded, and guarded in deep secrecy.

She filled her burrow–to add to her glory–
with berries of memory and seeds full of story,
and not just her own; from others she thieved.
"If my treasures live on, so will I," she believed.
When the moon hung one night like a great yellow gourd,
she ventured outside to add to her hoard.
With a whisper of wings, feathered death swooped in flight,
and *whoo-whoo-ah-whooed* as his talons gripped tight.

Fur pellets and bones of the Pack Rat, gone foul,
now crunch to the tread of the dread Great Horned Owl.

Storyteller Woman

*The Pueblo of Acoma sits atop a 367-foot, sheer-walled sandstone
bluff in central New Mexico. It is considered to be the longest
(since at least 1100 AD) continually inhabited community in North
America, and is known locally as Sky City.*

Gathered in Thanksgiving, our tribe
traveled to Sky City,
bringing Grandma, our Wise Woman,
to see lofty Acoma.
With eyes not yet dimmed,
she skimmed the chill horizon,
caught the lean of ladder
toward eternity.

Her cheeks grew pink above the fleecy shawl
that sheltered her from drafts.
When she heard that tribal homes
(since ancient times) are female-owned
and pass to youngest daughters,
she acknowledged with low laugh
her shared sisterhood with those faithful
keepers of hearth and family.

She believed, as they did,
in passing on her treasures–
those of legend, place, and story–
mother to daughter as a
sacred legacy.

FLY-IN AT THE BOSQUE DEL APACHE

*The Bosque (river forest) del Apache is a wildlife refuge and wetlands
on the Rio Grande in south central New Mexico. Near sunset,
thousands of birds return from daytime feeding grounds to the refuge
in an event called the "fly-in."*

The sun descends to rest on dimming shore,
as shallow waters wear a placid face.
Horizons holding back gray nimbus pour
their molten mercury in streams upon the lake
until the surface gleams. Adjacent moors
reflect metallic glows of sky and space.

As the refuge in the desert drifts toward sleep,
a gentle segregation flows among its guests.
Waterfowl divide by kind, as kindred keep
close to brothers, seeking sustenance and rest.
Among those who bear feathers, quarrels cease;
all shelter in the water when day shelters in the west.

Great blue heron, sentinel with spring-coiled neck,
strides on stately legs along the marsh.
Teals and mallards give their wings a final stretch
as sandhill cranes patrol where cover's sparse.
Dabbling ducks search shallows and green sedge;
wary snow geese land when skies grow almost dark.

Water all around fulfills a need
for waterfowl who gather in at night.
It wards against the hunter with four feet,
tan fur, long tail—whose yips sound out of sight.

The moat-surrounded flocks find safer sleep
than those who nest on land in dry moonlight.

ROUGH LANDING

From upper deck, I watched ducks congregate.
Some swam sensibly through reeds and sedge;
others gathered in the boat ramp parking lot.
Two drakes patrolled an ersatz puddle's edge,

a dent in asphalt covered by scant rain.
They dragged their bills to seine the shallow pond,
as if the inch-deep water hid some find.

I smiled inside, but those on whom I spied
looked at land-locked me and laughed outright.
Oh, some may claim that ducks say, *Quack, quack, quack,*
but what I heard was, *Hah-hah, hah-hah, hah!*

Your feet are poor for swimming without webbing;
your arms, unfeathered, are not suitable as wings.
Hah-hah, hah, oh poor, sad human being.

A female duck flew in to join her kind,
her angle steep. I winced to see her land,
skidding on the asphalt-masking shine.

Sister Duck, I cannot laugh at your distress,
for you braved flight, dared landing in a muddle.
I, too, have learned, when all I see is surface,
how hard it is to judge how deep the puddle.

If Winter Comes

The busy days of summer now are gone,
along with island tourists, who in droves
mosquito-like, buzzed over and upon
the Sanctuary's creeks and salty coves.

September starts the southward trek
of migratory birds, those pinioned swarms
who fly in echelons, with slender necks
outstretched toward the beckoning tropics' warmth.

The avian fall exodus is at its height,
in October's rustling, russet sheen,
as feathered Moseses guide winging flocks in flight
to promised lands of grain and grass and green.

Come November, just a hardy few are still
lingering to visit and to talk,
and share with me these days that turn to chill.
Soon, they'll journey with a larger flock.

Hollow reeds grow desiccant and fade
to dun and dull, then clatter in the breeze.
Even though we know what lies ahead,
we live these days and do not fear the freeze.

We trust that in the grasses' cyclic turn
from summer green, to autumn gold, to straw,
the wheel of nature's seasons will spin on,
and once again, in spring, shall come the thaw.

Progress Comes to Brigadoon-by-the-Sea

You knew the change would come
at the drawbridge on the bay,
when the tires' whine on causeway
over miles of reed-filled marsh
ended with a sudden, rumbling clank.

It meant that you were there,
when you heard those metal grates
scraping on decrepit concrete piers
and reached the creaky ramp
whose strongest fastenings
were rivets made of barnacles and prayer.

You chalked it up to progress
when the old bridge was condemned
by State Highways Division engineers.
You grudgingly accepted their new plan.
Now, an abandoned relic on the channel side,
the trestle rusts in salty, wind-blown spray.

Meanwhile, two hundred yards away,
a soaring, modern span
artfully dissects familiar sky
and dislocates your inner space
where gathered memories lie.

The old bridge was the checkpoint
where you shed the city's din,
became an Islander for just awhile, kin
to oysterers and watermen who range these shores,
following the paths of their forebears.

You wish it could remain unchanged,
this bay-and-ocean town,
where tidal rhythms mark the flow of time,
wild ponies graze on rough sawgrass,
your livelihood's the sea,
a weathered lighthouse guards
loblolly pines.

The dockside does look cleaner
since the trawlers moor elsewhere,
and fresh paint seems the rule all over town.
But, there's a sameness to the pleasure boats
now gliding down Queen Sound,
clever names inscribed upon their sterns.

The locals—when they christen boats—
choose names of family
to guard them as they make the turns
toward bright aisles of the sea.

TUNING THE HOUSE

This house, on stilts above the creek,
an orchestra, with reedy squeaks,
drumming tympani, and moans,
bells and whistles, flutelike tones,
cacophony that fills the hall
until the maestro's baton falls.
Sounds we do not recognize
bring to mind wild creatures' cries.

The south wind at the window screen—
could that be black wolf's lonely keen?
The scrape of chairs along the dock,
blown jaggedly on weathered boards—
or is it panther's hunting cough
just outside the sliding door?
From bedroom wing, a muffled crash—
a windblown wave, or cougar's slash?

Let's raise the window, change the tone
and make a whisper from a wail.
Let's tie the deck chairs to the rail
and cease to fret at the unknown.

This house needs no Beethoven's hand
to bring its timber into tune,
but just strong hearts. Strike up the band!
We'll play our fears behind the moon.

MUDBANK DINE AND DANCE

On Friday nights, you'll take a chance
if you go out to dine and dance
where denizens of salty deeps
(inhabitants of shallows, too)
gather 'mid the marshy reeds
in briny rendezvous.
Oh, the scandal that goes on
from down of day to up of dawn!

Sometimes the noise gets so loud
it drowns out the renditions
of Lawrence Whelk and his crowd
of bubble-prone musicians.
Crustacean ladies of the night
spin nautilus, exotic spells
and offer quite a stunning sight
when exiting their shells.

Not just shellfish are to blame;
bird-brained patrons act the same.
Loons go crooning at the moon
when overwrought and amorous.
Gulls recline upon the dunes
trying to look glamorous.
Opinions of what's too risque
seldom are unanimous.

When oysters get too boisterous
and crabs start waving pincers
when clams become too clamorous,

you'd best expect adventures.
The final straw—when drunks conch out
like flotsam on a barroom floor—
the hired mussel wades right in
and scallops them through swinging doors.

If you recoil at dives or fights
and have sweet visions of romance,
you'd best avoid those Friday nights
at the Mudbank Dine and Dance.

A Gentleman Would Not Notice

She is a pretty pier, a joyous jetty.
About her swirls a petti-
coat of briny waves and ruffled waters.
Along her sturdy decks,
moms visit with their daughters,
tourists walk their rhinestone-collared pets,
old couples stroll, young sweethearts kiss,
Grandpa teaches little hands to fish.

Wheeling overhead, gulls keep a wary eye,
swoop down for scraps the diners toss on high.
Visitors look up, and that's a courteous thing,
for like us all, this pier must face a reckoning.

At high tide, her coquetry is a song unbidden;
but when the tide begins to ebb, she dons a quiet air.
Don't disdain undainty feet, which aqueous skirts have hidden;
she has no pretty boots, but only barnacles to wear.

Hole in the Night

Stacked brick on brick on bands of red and white,
the Light stands sentinel across the bay.
A century and more of constant fight
against the whipping winds and swirling spray
have ribboned layers of once-bright paint
and dulled his armor. Yet, with mythic strength
he towers against a storm in summer's heat.
When the hearts of island folk grow faint,
he whirls his well-honed blade. Its shining length
slices lowering skies with steadfast beat.

The warrior taunts the foe, as thunder roils
and crawls the heavens with a fearsome crash.
From crowding clouds that sprawl in ragged coils
above the tossing woods, a jagged flash
arcs downward through the boiling, clashing dark,
just as the coward's arrow swiftly sped
across the battlefield of Troy so long ago
to strike Achilles–he of golden spark.
So also is the shaft of this age led
by fate to fell this hero, kill his glow.

Where the Light has held accustomed place,
now thrashing night contains a silent hole.
Dread rushes in to fill the trembling space
between the check of breath and chill of soul.
Though blinded, he still stands above the isle.
The intellect claims nothing is amiss,
sees no cause to fear for sightless portal,
argues that the void is but a while.

The heart, more truthful, finds in the abyss
the meaning of the designation *mortal*.

OLD SALT

Something in our bloodstream makes us hearken
to the song of lunar push and pull:
a gene of saline ancestry, a spark in
our souls when waves break deep and full.

We are our elemental tides, yearning to share
in ocean's amnion, earth's natal air.

Outward Bound

When cypress writhes before the unpacific storm,
when branches crack, saplings bend,
and gale-wracked junipers deform,
a champion is found to resist invader winds.
As clamor sounds among the vaults above,
One fortress species stands: the redwood grove.

Alone, a redwood's roots are thin beneath the forest floor,
but twined and interwoven, they seem to have no end.
Giants rise toward heaven from one close-netted core
anchored in community; each on each depends.
More than they are sheltered. Small species, too, abound
within their guardian branches; there, an ecosystem's found.

Can we, like the redwoods, let community arise
to cleanse and clear our planet, this nest that we've befouled;
extinguish all the burning of forest, sea, and skies
before we force sweet Gaia, in one last, desperate howl,
to sweep us from her body, like the vermin we've become?
What other world would have us, rejected by our own?

Fording the Styx

Our family played a game at night, as we drove into town
across the desert landscape, from north or west or east.
When waves of heat played tricks on sight beneath the August moon,
we saw our town a-twinkle by twenty miles at least,
lights doubled by mirage. We named it a lagoon.

But on one sunset journey home, we drove through clouds of dust
fender-high, tinged oxblood red when rays struck motes aslant.
No games dispelled these phantoms or chased away these ghosts,
remnants of a sandstorm, which, in its final rant,
whirled in waves, like tides of fire that lashed a rocky coast.

That night there was no banter, no games, and no pretense
as swirling, alien currents masked now-foreign shores.
We fought against believing we were held fast in suspense
over the Red Planet, named for the god of war,
or damned to watch dust devils dance

on Hades' flaming floor.

Palace Guard

When nights are lonely, deeply dark, and eerie,
with spouse away and neighbors out of reach,
I do not let my worries make me weary;
I trust my canine pals to guard my sleep.

My Labrador retrievers put to flight
imagined enemies–like sirens, owls, and cats.
With hackles raised, teeth bared, courageous hearts,
my dogs would give their lives–what loyal pets!

But when the thunder growls, they change their plan
to meet new circumstances (so I posit).
With common sense beyond mere mortal man,
they help me find the farthest corner of my closet.

PALEOMYTHIC

The dogs knew it first, begging
at the kitchen door to be let in.
Did their paws register subsonic vibrations,
scent-hound noses detect an ozone tang,
sensitive ears intercept signals
through tingling atmospheres?

We watched the electronic omens,
patches that grew red and scabbed,
like cankers, on the television screen.
They moved with the speed of contagion
while weathermen tried to reassure us
that the danger was remote.

Now, if you listen, other warnings sound.
The trunks of trees near ground
are still, but tops of cottonwoods
pass whispers to and fro,
afraid to speak aloud, as if their gossip could
make fear fact, just by saying so.

Enough of rumor—it's time for me to ascertain
what is ahead. I see curtains of rain
hanging from a proscenium of mountains.
Lightning glares in streaks and panes
at the base of the storm-swept range
like erratic footlights for an opera stage.

Distant tympani tune for the overture.
I tell myself my modern roof is strong,

close windows at the front of house and back,
then think of hail the size of marbles
coming down, battering a skylight marred
by one inconsequential crack.

Strange that, standing in this modern shelter,
I long for the surety of solid rock above,
limestone layering the dome of my snug cave,
where one narrow fissure in the roof
allows the smoke of our hearth fire
to find escape.

SCALES, FINS, FEATHERS, WINGS

Balancing Act

The day of my birth, September twenty-third,
the quadrisect of year, the cusp of change,
the autumn equinox just hours old.

The scales had barely tipped at my nativity.
Justice-wielding Libra ushered out idealist Virgo,
who exited my horoscope by one iota on the clock.

I imagine time so thin that taking one step back
would let me find my balance on the fulcrum,
would let me have a say which way to fall.

We have no voice in choosing natal stars
except for equinoxes every day:
moments we conceive the notion of our own rebirth,
perceive a shift of forces in the pivot point of fate.

SNAKE DANCE

In our pickup truck (so new that feline pawprints on its hood
can send us in a rush to the car wash down the street),
we keep the windows up to hush the grumble of the road,
the rumble of the diesel, and July Montana heat.
A bumper hitch behind, our tattered trailer comes in tow,
like a trolley—or caboose—in a Forties' picture show.

Inside the quad cab, heading for the Weiser Fiddle Fest,
in stereo surround, we hear the songs of yesterday:
a bit of bluegrass, Western swing, and then a change of pace,
Josh Groban singing melodies ethereal and fey.
As his voice ascends the heights, yearns for the blue sublime,
we enter a steep, winding gorge and downshift for the climb.

We round a curve, and suddenly (was it hiding all along?)
the Burlington Northern serpentines,
with too many cars to count or see where they might end,
each a vertebra that ripples down the anaconda spine.
In flowing locomotion, coiling through the channel's core,
the silver-scaled BNSF glides up the valley floor.

By the hands of puppeteers—the forgotten engineers
who years before laid down the roads and rails—
we are pulled into a *pas de deux*, a ballet of machines
partnered on a stage of rock and steel.
Truck and train sway, mesmerized, in courtship-ritual dance,
nearing, veering, drawn together, swept apart in swirling trance.

A tilt upends reality, time halts its forward sweep,
and gravity's a game of chance played on a roulette wheel;

but then, the spell is broken, as if a hypnotist
calls us back with finger snap into a world that's real.
The highway jerks us from the stage, swerves eastward on a plain.
In rear view, for an instant, we spot the westbound train.

FAMILY TREE

In the sunlit corner of Grandpa's
big backyard, beside the crooked
split-rail fence that runs along the creek,
stands the snag of a giant cottonwood,
old, older even than the grand
old man who, I surmised,
must have lived for centuries
to be so wise.

The gray, grooved bark folds deep
upon itself, peels away from the heart
in plates and creases,
like the scales and ragged scars
of an ancient dragon
that age has left both clever
and mysterious.

Gnarled limbs have vanished, one by one.
Grandpa sawed the deadwood flat
to stave off unrelenting fate.
But boughs were more accepting,
bowing to the call of time,
falling back to life-recycling soil.

Few limbs remain;
they no longer summon
leaves that, with the glowing
wand of autumn,
magicked into golden coins
cascading down,

piling in a dragon's hoard
heaped upon the ground.

No twigs remain aloft to snare
the flotsam blown about
by beckoning west winds.
Still, in the phantom branches
that shaded childhood realms
sticky tufts of memory cling and spin.

Scattered on the sun-bleached grass
like forgotten dreams, catkin
caterpillars undergo a wizard's spell,
bring forth enchanted butterflies
that flutter briefly in the light,
then, gently, wing
away.

CASTING FOR RAINBOWS

I've been around this lake a time or two,
prowled the depths beneath its sun-warmed
rocks, leapt its cascades, slept in its deep pools,
feasted on the breeding mayfly swarm.

I know the pattern of the light
as it shifts and prisms overhead,
and sends inconstant rainbows into flight,
while mine stay faithful, by my side.

I know where liquid Paradise abuts
the boundary of gasping Hell—how,
all along that edge, small insects flutter,
tempting the unwary fish who swims below.

From that canopy today, I hear
reverberations of a different kind,
the slap of water, but not water on a shore,
a scrape, a thud, a murmur (now, it ends).

Where ceiling dapples played, a shadow flows,
an eclipse darkening the sparkling dome.
Is it danger? All seems still. Should I stay, or go
out boldly to confront the lure of the unknown?

That filament of light has a peculiar slant,
an angle odd for this time of the year,
but see how, at its tip, the struggling nymph
wriggles upward to escape in sunlit air.

Obey caution, or strike hard and fast?
The choice takes but an instant, and my fate is cast.

A Fishy Story

I'm not much for eavesdroppin' at cowboy bars,
but one night at Jake's, a couple o' gents
got my attention. I perked up my ears
when they mentioned fishin', and here's how it went:

"Hey, Joe, I hear that they're starting to bite
at the 10-acre lake out on the King Ranch.
They tell me they've seen some mighty big pike
swimmin' just under that cottonwood branch."

"Well, Pete," Joe replied, "I *do* like to fish,
but somethin' that sticks in my craw
is how much *dinero* they think I should dish
out, for permits. There should be a law!"

"They have got a law," Pete said with a grin,
"It says if you ain't a-packin' a license
to show to the ranger, he'll take you right in."
Joe replied, "I'll just skip that expense."

"One permit's enough to keep two rods in play;
I'll just hold your extra, allowable line.
One angler, plus buddy along for the day—
who's to say different? Why, we'll be just fine."

According to rumor, a pike struck Joe's bait.
The battle was epic; but this tale gets stranger.
Joe landed the fish, but then, fickle fate
arrived in the guise of a young forest ranger.

Two weeks ago, *Rod and Reel* ran the story,
along with a photograph four columns wide,
of the prizewinning, trophy pike in all its glory,
with Pete at the scales and Joe off to the side.

Joe has been absent from public congrats;
I reckon he'll think twice before next he cheats.
One guess at whose name went into the stats,
for the fishin' was Joe's, but the license was Pete's.

Ichthyology

I live between an ocean of lush language
and a bay of beautiful words.

Each day, I cast my questing net
into the image-teeming sea,
hoping to pull on deck
a flashing, silver haul of similes
to be the envy of the fleet.

Though, bayside, I would be content
to reel in the wily metaphor
that swims just out of reach in the deep
hole—there, beneath the rock.

Some days my catch,
though meager and hard won,
is enough to still my hunger.

Some days, like other anglers,
I lament the behemoth
I brought so near the shore
from his lair out in the bay;
who, upon my glistening line,
wriggled in the sun
for a moment—just before
he kept the bait, spit out the hook,
and, once more, got away.

LOVE CALL

Gray-feathered clouds enshroud the early morning.
Across the tasseled grass and fading dew
drifts a wounded voice, "whoo-HOO-oo-oo,"
a haunting birdsong, wistful, low, and yearning.

Mourning doves–forever mates–
I wait to hear the partnered call
from splintered fence or crumbling wall,
distant willow, garden gate.

No still silhouette consoles my view.
Silence meets the lone refrain,
"whoo-HOO-oo-oo" intoned again.
Oh-WHERE-my love, are you?

In the tongue of doves, *love* is a word much spoken,
fidelity a vow that's kept lifelong;
but for the faithful creature, there is a final song:
the one who's left behind will croon, *Forsaken. Broken.*

La Paloma in Profile

Sweetness pervades the shape of a dove, in the
set of slender head on modest shoulders,
obedient sweep of back and breast,
compact body
that wastes no feather
on vulgar ostentation.

A gentle contour captures the heart,
as if purity of soul had found
its perfect demarcation,
as if we could share by tracing,
with compassionate hand or

yearning eye, the curve
from short, simple bill
past eyes of knowing surrender
toward folded wings ready to unfurl and
        bear an olive branch from beyond an ocean,
        flutter from smoke-stained battlements, or
        fly to unyielding stone
            atop high altars.

PHEASANT PRINCE

Strutting, bobbing in the tangled brush,
throat swathed in scarf of iridescent green
tucked into white collar. On his breast, a sheen
of houndstooth weave–a vest in red and rust.

The morning hour is misty, still, and dim.
The pheasant prince forgoes his raucous call.
I freeze in silence here behind the wall.
His sharp eyes know my eyes still follow him.

We are in accord, we early two.
He pretends he is not walking there,
I pretend I do not stalk or stare,
as I memorize each pose, each hue.

In some lands, pheasant is a prized entree;
on my land, he is entree into wonder.
It's sky and not cold glass he should be under.
I feast instead on beauty and stand sentry.

Mom Talks Turkey

Tom Turkey seemed, to me, Goliath-sized;
at four years old, I feared that tyrant bird.
He pecked bare toes and kept me terrorized.

My mom said, "Child, you'd better mark my word,
you cannot run from bullies. Here's the trick:
don't back down—prove *them* to be absurd."

I took my mom's advice, and found a stick,
set it by the door, where Tom stood guard.
At our next face-off, I got in first lick.

I chased that fowl all over our back yard.
Bullies are just weaklings dressed in lies.
To keep from being victim, strike back hard.

The trick's to find which stick will best chastise—
like truth, which strips the coward's thin disguise.

CRANES AT TWILIGHT, DANCING

Silhouetted cranes, in paired perfection,
stand backlit in the lakeshore's silver sheen,
stretch out bills to touch in shared reflection,
pose like dancers, settle feathers, preen.

Mirrored in the water's windless shimmer,
twinned birds now seem balanced by two more.
The quartet frames a patch of sunset glimmer
that floats between like polished ballroom floor.

Each spread-winged arabesque, each shift of stance,
each angled joint, each wingshake in the space,
each curve of neck, each head bowed in the dance,
creates kaleidoscopes of cosmic grace.

DAYLIGHT SAVING TIME

*"Let all men know how empty and worthless is the power of kings.
For there is none worthy of the name but God, who heaven, earth and
sea obey."*
—Attributed to King Canute the Great of Norway*

The clouds brought rain this morning.
At midday, they snowed blackbirds on the lawn.
Those princelings of the air, denied
their lofty perches, vainly stride,
stiff-legged on the streaming grass, cast
wary glances over gleaming shoulders.

The flock has been summarily dethroned
from its sagging realm of humming wires
by an upstart abacus of small, brown birds,
each usurper an unwitting bead
by which we count the wait until
the change of hands and change of hours.

A conspiracy of sodden skies
squanders daylight with a mob's abandon
and, unburdened with remorse or care,
strews darkness well before the slated hour.
No King Canute are the emperors of this age;
he bowed to limits on his mortal power.

Rulers who would boastfully command
that the celestial tide flow to their beat
are swallowed by their pride, left impotent.
No calendar, no clock, no edict of man

will keep the sun above the rim of day
or slow the swing of nature's pendulum.

*Canute's flattering courtiers had boasted that he was "So great he could command the sea." A religious man and clever politician who knew his limitations, Canute had his throne carried to the seashore, where he sat commanding the tide to come no further. When the water lapped around his feet, he had made his point that he would not be swayed by flattery.

WINDOWS OF THE SOUL

I ached to go to Mother as she died,
but my child's need for me surpassed my own.
So, I said goodbye by telephone,
unlike my sisters (four there, by her side).

They said Mom spoke a wisdom to each girl.
"What was her word for me before she went?"
but none recalled. I tried to be content,
but still I hoped—no, hungered—for my pearl.

An owl came to my window on a day
after we laid Mom beneath the grass.
We gazed at one another through the glass,
soul to soul, and then it flew away.

Her wisdom filled the eyes of that small bird
and spoke to me, at last, her parting word.

MOCKINGBIRD SUITE

I. *Allegro*
Shall I call you Captain Morgan of the Martin,
Buccaneer of Birdsong, Blackbeard of the Blackbird,
or River of the Wren?

Are you robber of the robin, thief of the gentle thrush?
Who would dare despoil your reputation,
when whispers of your prowess precipitate a hush?

Calico Jack of Sparrows, you need no others' words
to choir the treetop rigging. One order from your throat,
one note of bidding, sends aloft a hundred phantom birds.

With no nest-bound birth song, do you feel forsaken,
an orphan who must plunder sounding main
until you find a melody of your own making?

But what the harm, you say? The swallow keeps his art,
the warbler sings as warmly, the oriole still croons.
The treasure goes unburied—no need for secret chart.

I hope so, pirate songster. I, too, have stolen voices,
tried on couplet, sonnet, haiku, ode, quatrain
as if they were my own creations, my own choices.

Will we know our soul songs when we find them?
Do we search in vain?

II. *Andante*
Perhaps I wrong you with my human supposition,
impart low motives for your high-winged art.
You take no joy in simple depredation;
in nature's plan, you play a gentler part.

Yours is not the cruelty of the cuckoo,
who plunders others' nests to plant her chicks,
Yours is a kinder theft (oh, clever you!)
done with illusion, make-believe, and tricks.

Your warblings claim a hundred tiny fiefdoms,
as if each branch were home to a chorale,
and thus you steer away potential thieves from
the mansions of your meadowland locale.

For who could doubt when hearing such pure song
it came from other throat than it belonged?

III. *Largo*
Songsmith, welder of the lore of birds,
you meld into one lode the borrowed veins
of a hundred more whose strains would go unheard.

Amalgamated strands of molten ores
pour from your golden throat in swift cascade;
tones glow with fire in your incandescent forge.

Before the cock has roused himself to crow
the sleeping world's nocturnal dreams away,
you hammer silver cadences into their flow.

Incessant virtuoso, serenading night and day,
is there no pool of stillness, cooling dew,
where you can find respite and damp the blaze?

You toil with bursting breast and fervid zeal,
as if enjoined to store up in the now
a hoard of melody marked with your seal,

as if you see a future fashioned wrong,
when all other voices might be stopped, and you
alone remain, our only vault of song.

Coda
Your gift is the whole, not just the part,
no brief, compressed motif, but symphony,
your spirit the performer, accompanied by art,
to lift our hearts, transmit a mystery.
You have shown a better use of powers
by transcending stunted "Mine" for "Ours!"

TAKING FLIGHT

Tempus Fugit

Childhood hours flap on slow, crow's wings,
scribe circles in summertime's molasses-flowing air,
loop lazily on taffy-pulling noontides.

Prime time days of parenthood, tending children and careers,
pass in steady, migratory waves. V-shaped echelons
of dawn-to-dark scull steadily toward their autumn homes.

Weeks of elderhood in snow-blown fields
explode beneath the hiker's feet like frantic pheasants
that break from cover and blur noisily toward distant bracken.

WHITE FLIGHT

Inspired by Nancy Richards West's painting
of the same title, and the risks that she took for her art.

Face down on the fragile slab
of crack-scarred ice,
a meager skim on salt marsh pond,
the artist stretched full length
toward the crumpled heap
of feathers just beyond her reach:
an egret martyred to a February storm.

Heart fluttering, she prayed for strength,
then strained her painter's hand
toward immobile claws,
rejected the divide that yawned
between aspiring fingers
and the heron's pristine
grip on eternity and light.

An inch—immensity—measured the gap
between creation and creator-to-be,
like the image on the vaulted Sistine.
Yearning fingers touched at last;
with tiny strokes, she coaxed
the silent bird into her grasp.
It lay frigid, frost-eyed, still.

In thawing warmth of wood-fired stove,
she spread the rigid feathers,
careful not to bend against their will
the frozen wings, the hollow bones

like reeds–so light, so chill–
as she explored the articulation
of joint, frame, and pinion.

When, for her art and for a part
in beauty's resurrection,
she had garnered all this death could offer,
she opened up her water paints
to raise the regal bird aloft,
to give the world a way of seeing
both its inner and its outer being.

The egret's wings now span the Eastern Shore;
once again, white heron is aglow.
Its flight is pure, transcendent, more–
Rise, IceFire Phoenix, from your pyre of snow!

FUGITIVE

On seeing Salvadore Dali's painting, The Sacrament of the Last Supper,
at the National Gallery of Art in Washington, D.C.

Not even the curators, those experts on position,
could agree on a suitable place
to hang this surreal, too real Christ,
this in-your-face work of light and space
whose every line Dali had placed
so that the viewer's eye,
seeing the rendition of that final meal,
was drawn
toward the vortex of the known
but not yet signed and sealed.

Like an itinerant soul in witness protection,
it seemed to drift from one location
to another under cover of night.
For awhile, it graced, if not an upper room,
at least an elevated height
in the gift shop of the art museum,
until even the most obtuse
must have seen the irony
of silver changing hands to purchase
relics of man's dance with Deity.

It next appeared on the stairwell
where shuffling crowds transitioned
between the monstrous mobile
hanging like a rude
child's toy in the angled East Wing
and old rooms imbued

with Titian's heavy hues,
Rubens' corpulent nudes,
and luminous Dutch kitchens.

After the surfeit of cobalt, crimson, and gold,
Dali's placid blues and single touch of rose
were as incongruous as the Second Coming.

There, on that landing, as if released
from gravity, the iconic tableau
did not hang but float, incorporeal,
its geometry compelling as a spike,
inviting us to step from stairs through
canvas into sacrament and light.

But who knows what to do
with someone who portrays
a levitating rose in shades
of sepulcher and brothel
when he transfigures the ghastly
symmetry of destiny
into sweetness
so supernal
it brings us to
our knees.

BLUE AND GRAY

Warming sky of improbable blue. Manzano Range
a row of azure towers that ring the desert horizon,
their snowcaps shrunk to topmost slopes.
Rio Grande a dun runoff from spring's
sun-bathed, melting mountains.

On the bridge, a sideways glance
to gauge the flow against known levels,
and there, by chance, a heron: young,
slight frame, neck outstretched,
as if to sight tomorrow's
flight against the distance.

I have seen the Great Blue,
shoulders hunched by regal mantel,
promenade the green marsh stream,
make grand and stately entrance;
I have paid him the adulation due.

Drab fledgling, you have no cloak of royal blue
draped around your frame; you wear shabby gray.
So, why this shock as if you bore great beauty?
Is it the unexpectedness of you?
Is that what takes my breath away?

Running Before the Hunter

I run with gown aflutter toward my life's bright lover,
whose fragrant face, uncovered, I have yet to see.
My feet are wet with rose blood, stained with bruised red clover,
behind, I hear the tread of my pursuing enemy.

Not every truth is beauty–some hideous, some plain.
This truth wears scars of cold despair and flagrant mockery.
His visage I've confronted and, it seems, must face again,
for he returns to stalk my path relentlessly.

I had the courage in the past; I'll meet this present test
and if I fail at last, that day will not be this.
I try to sprint, increase my speed—he follows easily.

His hot, rapacious panting lifts hairs along my neck,
but I'll burst lungs before I'll bear the dismay of his kiss.
I'll leap the cliff before I'll let depression swallow me.

Morpheus Marooned

In the dreamscape on the other side of thought,
where creation hangs in timeless twilight,
I sing an epiphany in my true self's voice,
to rich orchestrations of my own composing.

My world is awash in a sea of poems;
perfect phrases float on tides of import.
Truth adorns herself in my utterance
and dances at my tongue's agility.

Words flutter at my mouth, moths dazzled at a screen;
their wings whisper secrets until, wearied, they go dumb.
Too soon, melodies recede toward distant mountains,
echoes seek seclusion in the island's muted caves.

The breaking day nags at the shutters of my eyes.
I grasp at chants and half-remembered spells,
try to pull them, whole and holy, through the net
of awakening. With tattered waves, they bid farewell.

The nocturnal seducer, god of sleep and dreams,
still beckons from the surf of his uncharted isle.
False-promise lips call to my departing sail,
"Come back, come back. . . ."

MAKING IT WORK

COVENANT

Should I look this Angel in the eye?
What if he be fearsome Gabriel,
announcer of great joy,
whose tidings loosed a virgin tongue
to sing, "My soul doth magnify. . ."
the self-same messenger who brooked no doubt,
and struck old Zechariah dumb?

Should I look this Angel in the eye?
What if he be cunning Lucifer,
renouncer of great joy,
whose urgings loosed a virgin mind
to taste the fruit of self-discovery,
who seceded from the realm of the Divine
by speaking his demands for parity?

Should I look this Angel in the eye?
Could I then inherit his fiery gaze?
Would I dare to utter his infernal
or his heavenly name if, in that decision,
I became consumed by the eternal,
or damned myself to burning in the blaze
of beholding with an Angel's vision?

If I looked this Angel in the eye
would my words be swept away,
become a torrent out of my control?
Would I then be forced to say
what hides within my virgin poet's soul?
I have no touchstone on which to rely,
should I look *this* Angel in the eye.

Quantum Theology

Every element of language is a form of some kind.
—Lewis Turco, *Book of Forms*

If poems were numbers and computers were infinite,
I would search for a magic algorithm of words
that—multiplied, magnified—would loop, swirl, and branch;
grow complexes of beauty; produce patterns truer
than I could devise but were there for the viewer.

I would pick random rhythms; make rules arbitrary;
press a key, set geometry free to take charge;
let order-willed Nature unleash her commands
so that language—awhirl, recombining, redundant—
might emerge, fully structured, from chaos and cant.

I would mix in a word full of color and curve,
like *cerulean*, cool blue, with slithering *C*,
lullaby *L*, and lingering *N*. Its vowels' soothing murmur
would bloom in bright hues, send tendrils to hang
over prism-edged consonants, softening their clang.

I could factor in lexicons; dress verses, like rooms,
with *objects d'art* from thesaurus and tome;
populate the equation with alliterative lists
full of fury and sound; let all self-rearrange
until meaning's observed and in that instant changed.

But, if reader-cryptographer (discoverer of truths)
should leap through my maze in intuitive quanta;
should find there a meaning perceived by his mind;

mistake mindless spinning for Wisdom Divine;
could I truly claim credit for the design?

I Got Here Backwards

"A serious girl," they said, as if they clapped,
And also, "She is wise beyond her years."
That sort of claptrap sure did keep me trapped,
Out of step with fashion and my peers.

Through teenage years, my pose was just a filler,
Mimicking my elders, mocking youth.
My classmates rocked and rolled, I chose Glen Miller,
Even said the Beatles were uncouth.

Since then, with evolution changing poesy,
It seemed I was the one most out of sync.
While *Slam* and *Feminism* passed right by me
I stuck to rhyme and rhythm with my ink.

But hope is here. This Goody Two Shoes has just learned
Formalism is now labeled as the *New Rebellion*.
Who would have thought 'twould take this long to earn
My secret wish: to be known as a hellion?

Wrestling Match
(with apologies to Erato)

The task was simple—just to write a sonnet,
but Inspiration dodged, then ducked for cover.
I mused, then thought, "I'll put my Muse right on it,"
and 'phoned Erato, "Hey, Babe, dash on over."

No coy mistress, she, but bellicose;
no simile caressed her lips or glance.
Before I had the chance to wax verbose,
she crouched behind the words in wrestler's stance.

She sprang at me in anapestic anger,
I responded with a spondee body slam;
when her metaphor half nelson spelled out danger,
I pinned her to the mat with five iambs.

She spat, "You know the throws, you've got the holds,
but, tell me, can you pen the poet's soul?"

A Question for Lorca

*The Duende, on the other hand, will not approach at all if he does
not see the possibility of death...if there is not every assurance he can
rustle the branches borne aloft by us all, that neither have, nor may
ever have, the power to console.*
—Federico Garcia Lorca, *Buenos Aires, 1933*

Suppose that, in a redwood grove,
one young tree, latent
with a treasure trove
of angel-given grace,
plus the blessing of a Muse,
aspired to a great, green height.

And suppose she hearkened
to the ancients' advice
concerning how to find one's poems—
the lore that passed from branch
to crowning branch
in the leafy diadem dividing
elemental earth from fragile sky.

Suppose the tree (strong,
straight, and slender) sent roots
searching, honestly courageous,
despite warnings she must brave
the brink of self-extinction,
dare *duende* to find her prophetic voice.

Suppose her questing roots found
a recess in the earth, deserted

by the goblins who, legend said,
would dwell therein forever, and

the sluggish cesspool
that once drained this cave of pain
had cleansed itself and now ran free,
feeding a stream of diamond clarity.

Having dared so fiercely
to achieve her destiny, would she
now feel cheated or betrayed?
Could she trust the newfound
knowledge of her heart?

How would she tell this vision
to those whose art was purchased,
so they claimed, by resurrecting hell?

If dancing with demons
were the sole accepted way
to ecstasy, what then?
What, then, could she say?

Buy the Farm, Bite the Dust, Kick the Bucket

It was a dark and stormy night, and poet Thomas Gray
was knocking at death's doorstep, big as life.
Not to beat around the bush, he'd said his last hurrah;
to call a spade a spade, Tom skated on thin ice.

Just fallen off the turnip truck, he mistook the House of Tomes
for libraries he had known since callow youth.
But, as luck would have it, in its halls assassins roamed;
there, similes as old as dirt still ruled the roost.

He stopped to smell the roses in a room marked *Genteel Verse*;
that was the straw that broke the camel's back.
For my two cents, his fortunes took a turn much for the worse—
death and destruction lurked, unnoticed, in the racks.

Green-eyed monsters on the shelf, too numerous to mention,
pelted him with everything but kitchen sink.
The road to Hell, they say, is paved with good intentions;
down and dirty gets you there quicker than a wink.

You can bet your bottom dollar metaphors beyond the pale
bellowed like bulls in a china shop,
then drove poor Thomas up a wall 'til he was dead as a doornail.
For them, it was as easy as falling off a log.

An armchair quarterback would say Tom took one for the team,
while the culprits, thick as thieves, all flew the coop.
Better late than never, the cops jumped in with both feet
and left no stone unturned in hot pursuit.

Will wonders never cease, they caught the "perps" redhanded;
put the accused 'twixt rock and harder place.
A judge–the real McCoy–to whose court the trial's remanded
says, "Theirs to pay the piper; fat chance they get to first base."

Justice is blind as a bat; the jury is still out,
though we trust that every dog will have its day.
But the moral of the story is, whenever you're in doubt,
avoid like plague, the murderous cliché.

THE MAN WHO BROUGHT LIGHTNING TO EARTH
(Nikola Tesla, 1856-1943)

To uncoil the bonds of the static

electrify the imagination

shape the aura of sound

find the art beyond articulation

embrace the inaudible metaphor

comprehend the whole
     generated by a word

light the spark of speech and
     transmit it through a void

look into the heart
     of matter, feel its blaze

image an invisible world,
     launch it on phantom waves

see a current, its direction,
     conceive its alternate

speak out boldly, brave ridicule,
     die proud, but a pauper

You, Nikola, the wireless poet!

Frau Einstein Pours Tea

Forgive my son, dear neighbor, if he seems
disinclined to join your children in their games.
A good boy, certainly, but we admit
that Albert's head is filled with strange imaginings,
a silliness of numbers, the night sky's turning,
other diversions he regards
with childlike gravity.

His father and I fear he is slow,
for he lacks the aptitude or wit
most youngsters show
for even the most ordinary learning.
He always seems to be adrift
in his own dimension. It's as if
he wanders in a different time and space.

We can only pray
that he will someday find a place
where others will be relatively kind
to one of such a slow
but gentle turn of mind.

MNEMOSYNE DOES PARTICLE PHYSICS

Keep your eye on an anion
in a changeable mode,
for it might migrate quietly
to another anode.

Don't let it get nervous
or leave it at large,
for it's positively jumpy
when negatively charged.

A cation moves like
a static-filled kitty
with positive attitude
though it's itty bitty.

Like some Puss in Boots,
to cathode it swaggers,
inclined to transmute
any metallic laggards.

ISOSCELES

A
Tip
Of ice
Hints at
Icy doom,
Lurks, cold,
'Mid the gloom
Of mid-Atlantic.
And it sinks a ship
That had been called
Unsinkable–epic, bold
Titanic. Under the waves,
The iceberg held this shape.
The same traces hard outlines
Around All-Seeing Eyes, defines
The stacked stones of the Pyramids
Stepping Egypt's skies. In a Christian
Frame, it is a symbol of the Trinity. With
Three sides enclosing three angles, to some,
Triangle says *stability*. To those who watched
The wedged prow of Titanic sink beneath the sea,
How did the shape appear? Did those on board sing
Triad chords as they hymned *Nearer, My God, to Thee*?

EUCLID, AT THE GYM

Hypothesis:
    If   you hope the perfect form or figure to regain,
    Then   you must be ready to endure the certain pain.

Proof:
Triangular as the Greek letter that became their sobriquet,
my deltoid muscles ride heavily, like leaden epaulettes
on shoulders that I should have given more consideration.

Upon my back, I wear a groaning yoke of broad, flat traps.
Had I waited on those weights and exercised discretion,
a trapezoid of soreness would not sit where it's positioned.

Rhomboids rumble anxiously just beneath the scaps,
lined up, oblique and parallel, in multiple divisions.
I guess that I invited Hell with all those repetitions.

Corollary:
    If   you try to get in shape by clinging to taxonomy,
    Then   you run a solid risk of learning plane geometry.

SLIPPERY SLOPE

Those learned folk who write
for *The Philosophers' Review*
have explained most carefully
the fallacy of thinking
that a single rock clattering
down a slope would
inevitably
send all the others scattering
and strew them mathematically.

Surely, one stalwart stone would cling
to its place, its foundation being
buried in a firmer, deeper space.

Nor would a tree, toppling
from a great, green height
bring down many others,
necessarily,
even if, with 95 percent accuracy,
it struck its forest brothers.

Surely, some would stand and more rebound–
those younger, stronger hearted might
be rooted in the bedrock farther down.

And, as for that hapless dromedary
who is just following his nose
until he finds a tent flap
temporarily unclosed,
perhaps he would not like what he saw

within, would withdraw
voluntarily.

Surely, someone would dissuade
the thoughtless beast
from wandering in to overrun the feast.

As here, among the canvas folds
of our philosophy, we take our repose,
we see we have an uninvited guest.

What heresy is this, what bold
and questing bulge against the flap?
How impudent!
But who will turn away
this surly pest?

Surely, someone else
in this host will do what's best, will slap
that camel's nose.

Surely, someone in this tent . . .

TOOLS OF THE TRADE

After supper, at the settling of night,
hours past the hour his own crew went home,
Dad would go back to the building site.
Sometimes, he would let me go along.

How I loved to see his hammer, saw, and rule
conspire in building cabinets–custom made.
From the careful way Dad handled all his tools,
I learned more than how he plied his trade.

He taught me to be thrifty but not cheap,
insisted every measurement be square.
He built with birch and maple woods,
whose grains ran true and deep,
no second-rate materials hidden by veneer.

He said that cutting corners
would always boomerang,
just like spreading gossip
would bring the speaker pain.

Then, as if to test me, he would swear
me to secrecy and then would share
his opinion of those customers
who always changed their minds.

"That gal wonders why I charged an extra fee,
but she's had me move that closet two times–no, it's three!
Honey, think things through, don't just decide;
but once you've made your choice, let it ride."

I watched Dad building cabinets,
building windows, building doors,
building trust between us,
building honor,
building more.

A Woman's Work

Soundbound

I rise with birds of dawn, to seek the solitary hour
sanity craves before the daily sentence starts again.
I hear the whispered hope of steam in kettle,
bubbles rock against the stainless steel.

The tea is scalding in my cup.
High in my nose, I taste its fresh perfume.
It is criminal to forsake its silken bergamot
so soon to brew the black, strong coffee
the ancient crone, now my obligation,
learned to drink on graveyard at the depot.

Even now the brew, with a night of sleep,
gives her, for an hour or so, a cogent mind
and something of her memory of old.

I cling to this aria of peace, which briefly plays
until another theme creeps in–
discordant percussions are the herald
of beginning and of end–
shuffle flop of slippers, fleece-lined feet on tile
shut-shut, shut-shut, shut-shut.

Break of day or a sense of those astir
has roused her from her bed.
The scuff of sound warns of her approach.
Shut-shut and I stoop out of sight,
knowing that her failing ears
can't record my guilty flight.

Too soon, I must play warden.
I must invoke the vigilant eye;
keep her car keys high, out of her reach;
give plausible excuses, reasons for delay
in letting her return to live alone
in the home she's known for fifty years–
her sanctuary, where she is no longer safe.

With Doppler finely tuned to the juggernaut
shut-shut, shut-shut, shut-shut
chugging without letup toward my day,
I once more steel myself to play
out our mutual sentence. How long
will I serve as jailer, fugitive, prisoner–
here, in my own home?

COVER-UP

She laid cold veneers over
the reality she was born into,
wore the mask of gentility,
wielded etiquette like a whip,
doctrine like a cleaver.

She lived the denial
until she became it, believed it
in the reaches of her heart,
ingrained it in the synapses of brain,
trained and drilled to make
polite responses automatic.

Like a spy whose public life is just a cover,
she inhabits a shadow land of deception
where she has kept,
like a ruinous state secret,
the story of a love found and forbidden,
a heartbreak she will not chance again.

She keeps her vow of silence wrapped
in blankets of rectitude
and daily rites of obligation.

But now, as rebellious
layers of remembrance
surge and peel and crackle,
she no longer has the steel
or the tools to mend and plaster,

nor the jailer's keys
to imprison what was real.

It is coming back as dreams,
only to be labeled as delusion.
But she would want it that way–
to take the truth into oblivion
undiscovered, unrevealed.

CRACKED WOMAN

Her mind is   a mirror, shattered,
   a child's   toy box of
   scattered   fragments
and pieces   that no
   longer   fit,
just a   tumbled
down,   jumbled
      up   jig-
      saw   of
      memory   and wit.
      Doggedly,   she tries
      to frame,   rearrange
      all the   Tinker-
         Toy   bits,
         over   and
      over   and
   over,   and
over,   and. . .
hoping   *deja vu*,
relentless   repeating,
   fleeting   dreams
   that seem
   real, or
reality   that
   seems   dream,
   or reality that is in
         fact, fact,
            can pull to-
         gether   the
            tat-ters, knit
      known pat-terns
            so   the
               whirl
                  will
                  quit.

At the Motor Vehicle Department

I first came here to put an end
to her beloved driving,
this 89-year-old who insisted
she saw trucks that were not there,
but could not hear the wail
of the ambulance that passed us on the hill.

She said her "walker's I.D."
was a lousy trade at best
for the license that enabled her
to drive from coast to coast.
I was willing to weather her anger
to prevent those other likely dangers.

My second venture here, I came alone
for the dangling placard with its
stylized wheelchair logo.
The preferential parking was a sop
to mask restriction with civility
while exposing her infirmities.

For this third round, I have debated
whether to renew a pass soon slated to expire,
for she seldom gets out anymore.
"Long drives just confuse your mother,
and she gets so tired," report the aides
who watch over her where she resides.

Only in the waiting
does she not grow weary.

They say she sits out in the vestibule for hours
waiting for the bus "to take her to the coast,"
waiting for the train "to pull into this station,"
waiting for her mom "to take her on vacation."

I sit like others in this purgatory,
resignation weighing on our shoulders,
I think of her, two miles away,
and shudder at the irony of language.
Different? Yes, we are,
but in this we share: we're
waiting for our number to be called,
waiting for renewal to begin.

THE REFUGE FOR DISTRACTED LADIES

The hearing aids do nothing for
her 90-year-old ears,
she insists (or swears
that wearing only one
works so much better).

She does not dare
augment the static
that crackles from star
to star in the universe
between her left ear and her right.

Besides, every whisper
that hisses across
the ether of her worlds is amplified,
here in *les jardins*
of *Le Roi* Louis Sixteen.

So, she perches quietly
on a chair of damask *fleurs-de-lys*
and, in prim delight,
takes tea
with Queen Marie.

PARDON

I wed her son, sought to be daughter,
but I soon discerned the truth;
she was loathe to play Naomi,
I, reluctant to be Ruth.

She ruled as if she were a monarch,
with family bowing to demands.
For forty years, I waited, silent,
as she issued her commands.

Now I tell her, "Put your coat on.
Come this way. Sit down and eat."
To her, these words spell insurrection,
to me, a charge that I must keep.

Sight and hearing (ninety years' worth)
dimming now, but what's unkind
above all else is the unwinding
of a once bright, nimble mind.

In God's mercy, what's the reason
that she must live on in pain,
without eyes, ears, understanding?
What's the lesson to be gained?

Are these years a purgatory
meant for her–or meant for me–
to learn compassion, forsake rancor,
find the path to amity?

At the start, I burned in anger;
slowly, my heart's turned toward trust.
So, she'll go with my true blessing
when her dust returns to dust.

Postlude

All agreed it was a blessing,
gave thanks that, when it arrived,
it was peaceful and swift.
Heart ruled over head, at last,
foiling dementia's cruel slide.

A life and all its seasons
celebrated with full honors,
and the guilt for wishing that
her body not survive
her mind's demise
will diminish,
given time and reason.

The courtesies are done,
thanks said to the proper people,
forms and rites fulfilled,
phone calls of appreciation,
all required notifications.

Where there was
hypervigilance and stress
there is now an easing
of tight shoulders, grief
softened by relief,
gratitude for grace,
but not yet self-forgiveness.

We focus on tasks
that must be done

by those still living.
We pass her empty room,
silently sidestepping her absence,
which persists at every turn.

SABBATICAL

Desert dwellers know the keeping of a well,
its preservation through the generations,
the years that are for drawing and for drinking,
the seasons of replenishment and rest.

O my sister, you have hauled the jar of water
for many wayfarers, their flocks and herds;
you have poured the cup for thirsty travelers,
bade them to your fire, shared your bread.

But even a great lake can be made muddy
if all who need to drink crowd on its shores.
Let your neighbor, also, host the sojourner
and share the joy of giving without stint.

The Divine has given us a respite
to refresh our wellsprings and our souls.
The seventh year should not pass by unseen,
like a cutpurse in the stalls of the bazaar.

Let the cistern of your spirit be refilled
at the fountain of your heart's Creator,
so that, come next year–or year beyond–
you will once again stand like a green oasis,

beckoning to those who cross the wastelands,
made ready for the weary who need rest.
We cannot nourish others from our dearth.
Tend your well, dear sister, tend your well.

PHILODENDRON CORDATUM

When my sister Gwyn was born,
fifth daughter and last child,
Mom's best friend gave her a glossy
heart-leaf philodendron.

It thrived, as houseplants seemed obliged to do
in Mother's care, inhabiting a modest pot
circled by green ceramic leaves
(Art imitating Nature).

In Costa Rica, philodendrons grow huge
in perpetual eclipse on the jungle floor,
saucer-sized leaves cupping every mote of light
that penetrates the canopy.

What is it like to grow in the shade
of older siblings? To find, when the
sun's rays finally filter through,
that the trees have grown old?

To the Gender Feminists
(To Make Much of, if They Wish)

I received my senior high diploma
about the time that *Feminine Mystique* came out.
It would have taken being in a coma
not to know what all the shouting was about.

My college friends preached feminine resistance,
urged me to burn my bra–they'd lend assistance!
Chauvinism? What was that to me?
The tyrant I knew best was poverty.

At nights I waited tables at the truck stop.
I had a choice: tuition or vacation.
My father worked until he nearly dropped

to see five daughters got an education.
So, every man's a beast? Exclude my Pop.
His belief that I should fly–my liberation.

Extreme Makeover

For 50 plus years my nose slid to the left
down the side of my face to a lip that was cleft.
But the day finally came when I came into money,
and I said to myself, "The time has come, Honey,

to put that nose back where it should have been
and turn lopsided smile to symmetrical grin."
If I were going to go under the knife,
why not erase other signs of long life?

So, I talked it over with my plastic surgeon,
and he agreed without too much urging;
we added some snips, some nips, and some tucks.
It's amazing how smart you can get for big bucks.

I can think of no other way to explain
the attributes for which I have since won acclaim.
Folks sought my wisdom, my talents improved,
though I cannot fathom how that change evolved.

My I.Q. expanded, it hit a growth spurt,
I suddenly had keen perception.
I'd not noticed before how old men loved to flirt,
nor been given such friendly reception.

Gents who, in past, spared a nod or a shrug
or by whom I was simply ignored,
now called me *Darlin'* then asked for a hug
and hung upon my every word.

Why did my old habits gain new applause,
and how did my jokes all get wittier?
Surely, it cannot be simply because
my engineered features are prettier.

Beauty's skin deep, so I've heard all my life,
but that was before I went under the knife.
We think we're so great at seeing what worth is,
but we all judge each other by what's on the surface.

Just the FAQs, Ma'am

Consider the spider and her web,
the tensile strength
of one slender filament cast into the wind,
the vast chasm between
wall and adjoining gate
where she anchors the silky strand:
a great distance, as if a woman had flung
a stone across a river and knew the tug
of its anchoring beyond the arc of sight.

Consider the intelligence required
to guide each leg in the purposeful
patternmaking of a geometric orb,
or to hold perfectly still, silent, patient,
waiting like the funnel spider, at the rear
of a loose web, deceptively disarrayed,
but sufficiently structured to telegraph
telltale oscillations from thin tripwires.

Consider the materials of the arachnid's trade:
the sticky bola swung
to lasso those with wings,
the viscous ladder whose rungs
capture careless moths,
the resilient net held in the pedipalps,
poised to be flung
over fleeing prey,

the nocturnal tent struck
at first glint of dawn,

the shimmering lure from spinnerets,
the swaddling of egg sacs
securely wrapped,
the clever trap-
door level with the sands;
consider these handy tools
extruded from a self-reliant body.

Consider the solitary spiders:
the widow, the brown recluse;
the cryptic tarantula who, upon retiring,
puts a silken welcome mat outside his den.
Consider battles in the desert, unseen,
between belly-barbed arachnid and
determined tarantula hawk,
(giant wasp who earns her sobriquet
in the pursuit of her favorite prey);
consider the outcome of their lethal ballet,
as she seeks to transform him with one sting
into a living nursery for her young.

Consider why we humans see the web,
in legend and in lore as symbol
of illusion or intrigue,
then seek to weave
ourselves into a worldwide web;
why we colonize the ether
through leagues of website "Friends,"
why "web crawler" is the name
for spies we send searching incessantly
for information and connection.

Consider why the Web

is now our oracle, wherein
we seek to sort out truth
from magic, myth, and fear;
why two Frequently Asked Questions are:

Why do female spiders eat their mates?
Can male spiders spin?

Moorings

Her hands no longer move with youthful grace;
their knotted knuckles, threads of thin, blue veins
reveal the years gone by. But in the place
of nimbleness, old mastery remains.

Stiff fingers grasp the flashing, slim harpoon
of needle, lay down lashings stitch by stitch
in perfect rows of three. She hums a tune
to weave the binding spell, the one from which

no strand can pull away. She hides the seams
as she was taught while dwelling with the elves,
when she untied her sailor's restless dreams
and tethered their frayed moorings to herself.

His unspent wanderlust, securely sewn
inside her pillow, serves as love's headstone.

THE HOOVER SOUL SEARCHER EZ-3

Each purchase comes fully equipped

with convenient crevice tool
    to suction out hidden recesses
    where carcasses of regret collect
    between baseboards and rugs
    you've tried to sweep them under

with rotary upholstery brush
    to agitate the fibers of memory,
    lift old residues of resentment
    to the surface, and filter them
    into disposable canisters

with short-handled stair sweeper
    for easy cleanup of intolerance
    as the user progresses
    from lower landings of judgment
    to upper stories of compassion.

Limited warranty.
Not responsible for deliberate misuse.

Epitaph

Everybody says (in memoriam),

"Beloved wife, mother, sister, friend."
Some, if they are fortunate,
are remembered for gifts
that brightened their world:
"Musician, Gardener, Author, Artist."

Nobody says (in memoriam),

"Here lies a superb duster of furniture,
a faithful scrubber of floors,
an accomplished
organizer of closets."

Knowing this to be so,
on those days when I have a choice
to leave as my legacy
sparkling toilets and folded clothes or
a sonnet that holds
a fragment of soul,

I shall choose to write poetry.

WARD ROBE
–Don we now our gay apparel

To ward my soul, I'll sing bright melodies,
inhale the breath of bursting springtime sky,
step to a beat (head high), fling my arms wide,
to mirrored eyes, chant charms for bravery.

I'll choose the skirt that flows in silken rustles,
wear shoes of Spanish leather, serpent-supple,
their weight a bluebird's feather. I will dance
a tarantella to elude the black romance.

I'll take what's reachable near closet doors.
I will not rouse the deeper, brooding rods
where winter sighs through shawls of musty wool,

old coats don hoods like scowling monks, mute scarves
long to wreathe my throat in gallows' knot
or serve as blindfold when the trapdoor's–pulled.

THE DARK MONTH

Through this black December,
I will remember that,
though the light is fading,
and for some may not rekindle,
inevitably a flame
will blaze on the horizon.

Despite this sky of frozen jet, which mutes
the roar of churning solar furnaces
whose warmth traverses galaxies,
I will recall that, even at the universe's edge,
crystal pinpoints shine in silent promise,
faces turn toward the stellar light of summer.

And in this month of glacial hope,
when nights stretch to a year,
I will carry sparkling candles,
have matches at the ready,
rejoice with the evergreen and the
scarlet cardinal defying the snow.

Moon of the Huntress

Countenance of spectral white
screened by frozen mist,
lunar lantern rays aslant,
vectors on an icy axis,
clouds spun like spider strands
on a crystal lattice,
the sharp scent
of tinkling snow,
and, on the tongue,
the knife-edge tang
of angular flint.

Ruler of this precise sky
is Greek Artemis:
bringer of order,
warder of virtue,
defender of wild things,
huntress.

Suddenly, a barking of hounds
and the sparkling sky yields.
A wheel of wantonness gains speed.
On this untamed
side of midnight,
the moon goddess dons
the Roman dress, face, and arms
of virginal and strong
Diana, women's
sometime protector.

I seek shelter in her shield's
full circle; find only
the arc of a bow,
the curve of an antler,
the crescent call
of a waning, distant horn.

SANCTUARY

The casement casts a splotch of light
upon the windswept lawn;
the ocher cuts the darkling night
and spreads its shadow spawn,
frail phantoms of distorted sight
that dread the distant dawn.

Inside, my dear, the lamp shines bright.
I think we'd best stay in tonight.

The dogs are baying in the West;
their howls float on the wind
that withers reeds at river's edge.
What does its chill portend?
No night bird trills from her soft nest;
how will her silence end?

Inside, my dear, the lamp shines bright.
I think we'd best stay in tonight.

The firewood grows small, my dear.
No! Do not go for more.
I cannot see the sounds I hear
a few feet from the door.
If you go out, I truly fear
you'll come to me no more.

Inside, my dear, the lamp shines bright.
I think we'd best stay in tonight.

CROSSING BOUNDARIES

VENUS, RISING

I could have floated forever
in this tranquil and virginal sea,
slept in its sapphire cradle
untroubled by lust's urgency

had Vulcan not roused me from slumber,
his lava kiss sizzling the foam,
his summoning song of desire
flowing out from his fiery home.

What fanned my heedless abandon,
made me rise to tumultuous air,
forsake my blue spread of deep ocean
for his crimson bed, as I dared?

How could I resist the blaze burning,
though I could not name its true source,
nor what in my body was yearning
to melt in the glow of the forge?

From that day when the fire was ignited,
the impulses driving me surged.
In hammering of heart I delighted,
to anvil of love I emerged.

CASKET DOWRY

*In the early 1700s, the French king sent young women to the New
World to become colonists' wives. Their royally supplied dowries (or,
"marriage portions") consisted of household goods packed in coffin-
shaped crates (baskets). Thus, the nickname "casket girls" for these
women given "basket fortunes."*

I am called "casket girl," but my name is Yvette.
A ward of the king, I have come to your shore
from Provence, where I was left orphaned and poor,
though I kept my honor, a true *fille a' la cassette.*

All that I own is what I can carry
in this coffin-shaped basket of linens and clothes,
which does not speak death, as you might suppose,
for it holds my dowry. I've come here to marry.

You colonists need us to work by your side
as you claim the Southland of this continent.
In New Orleans, Biloxi, wherever we're sent,
our progeny someday will claim us with pride.

I'll help build this nation as my gift and portion.
I bring you, though meager, no mean basket fortune.

Frontier Wedding

Sometimes we may wonder about folks back yonder,
especially our kith and our kin.
This story's been told to all young and old
in this clan, but let's tell it again—
how Grandpa Ken and Grandma Veo eloped.
In the Year '43 it began.

"Arizona," Ken said, "has a whole three-day wait,
and three days can cut like a knife.
Across the state line, a county seat will do fine
as the place to start our married life.
In Reserve, there's no waiting; I'm anticipating
tomorrow we'll be man and wife."

So, they drove all that night, and by dawn's early light
reached Reserve, in the pine-covered hills.
For their morning repast "What is open?" they asked
and were told, "Uncle Bill's Bar and Grill."
Ken stepped into the bar to buy a cigar
and to pay for their just finished meals.

There, he told a refined co-stander in line,
"Your cigar is on me, my good chum,
for today I'll be wed." "Is that so?" the man said,
"Then you'll need my help getting it done.
It's the weekend, you know, and the courthouse is closed,
what is more, county clerk's out of town."

"The license you crave will be locked in the safe,
but you'll need it right there in your hand.

However, take heart, I'm the sheriff in these parts
and I think I may just have a plan.
A burgler's the chap, he can make this day happy
a safe cracker–I know just the man!"

So, the sheriff went to look for the just-paroled crook.
This notion gave Veo a start.
Of course she was frantic, but it got real romantic
when Ken said, "You've stolen my heart,
so this way is fitting for our nuptial knitting,
and with this guy, it's almost fine art."

And so, they gained entry while the sheriff stood sentry,
found a license they signed in a hurry,
called up a justice of the peace and said, "Trust us,
we're bound and determined to marry."
"If today's when you're wishing," he said, "I'm going fishing,
so, come now; you'd better not tarry."

Both sides of the law helped to hitch Ma and Pa
for 50 plus years, and I'm betting
this tale matrimonial is a fine testimonial
to a moral we'll ne'er be forgetting:
true love conquered all in what they came to call
their genuine, frontier-style wedding.

Bone Orchard Oath

(bone orchard: A slang name for a cemetery.
–Ramon Adams' Western Words, A Dictionary of the Range, Cow
Camps, and Trail, 1946)

A young drover died on the ol' Chisholm Trail
while the herd pushed toward Abilene.
"Where shall we plant him?" his *compadres* asked.
"Somewheres with a small touch o' green,
and mebbe a tree or a bush to give shade,
fer he said, where he come from, trees covered with moss
grew by cricks in what he called a *glade*,"
answered the grizzled Trail Boss.

The cowpokes who buried him said, " 'Tis our loss.
The kid pulled his weight, didn't cheat, didn't lie,
and kept hisself cheerful to boot,
shared with his saddlemates, cared fer his hoss.
As we lay him to rest 'neath the blue Western sky,
let us swear to bear similar fruit."

COOKY'S STEW
for Howard Termain (1936 - 2003)

First, you heat your kettle on a medium flame;
then, take out your cut o' meat or your cut o' game.
Life's a cowboy cook-off, you seldom get to choose
your favorite ingredients; what you get is what you use.
And if that hunk o' elk or beef looks like it's kinda tough,
any cook who's worth his salt can put it right enough.

Put tenderizer on each side. A pinch or two will do
(a smile, a joke, a knowing hug), how much is up to you.
Dust on some compassion, and fry it quick in lard
rendered from a workday that was long and hot and hard.
Stand right there beside the fire, keep stirrin' at the pot;
can't give this chore to someone else just 'cause the campsite's hot.

Sear until the juice locks in—it's your fault if it burns.
A man gets back what he puts in; he lives, he grows, he learns.
Ya gotta add some onions, though with peelin' you'll be weepin',
but if you ain't cried, you ain't tried, and that life ain't worth keepin'.
Add 'taters, too, a humble root, but like a steadfast friend,
they'll stick by you and see you through until the journey's end.

The next part is where chefs are made—when all begins to bubble,
add some spice from a well-lived life, complete with joy and trouble.
Every cook's got a special blend that makes it all his own.
Cooky's herbs were earthy, hearty, and home-grown.
The hardest part (to set the lid, sit back, and let it simmer)
takes know-how, faith, and patience to serve up a real winner.

Cooky walked in honesty and served as he was able.
You ask my view, his campfire stew graces Heaven's table.

INSURRECTION

"Two roads diverged in a wood, and I–
I took the one less traveled by"
–Robert Frost

Her sneakers knew the road taken
so often that its curves were in their creases;
they remembered all the signposts, hedges,
fences, barriers, bridges,
and precisely numbered paces.

The repeated rise and fall of jogging ritual
conformed her feet this way or that,
ruled the slant of cushioned soles,
adjusted pressure on the tongue,
kept tight the knotted laces.

She could have run it blind
in those shoes. Ingrained in their leather
were the habits formed for every stretch,
there to soothe a restless mind,
and enforce the tracks, the traces.

Perhaps it was the loosing of a final leaf,
the scarlet letting go of summer vision,
the notion that approaching winter eves
would wrap about her a cocoon
of enforced introspection.

In her November hands there lay
the rebel force, the arms, the ammunition:

new shoes to run a separate way
(perhaps to travel there with a companion).
And so was born a revolution.

The thought of unknown roads ahead
caught at her throat, unbidden.
Finding her own feet and heart
would take some courage on her part,
as would running on a path less trodden.

CAUTIONARY TALE

Maybe I can stand on my head.
Maybe it would help the blood
to flow in my brain, stir creative eddies
where inspiration now seems mired in the mud.

On second thought, it might be tough
on my neck, given that I suffer whiplash,
and who knows what my old dog
might do if I came down in sudden crash?

We've been here before, my fears and I,
debating the next step, weighing its cost:
e.g., *Maybe I should loose my words to fly,*
but then, a better phrasing might be lost.

"Just inside that cave are gold and gems so bright
they shine like fire," I was told when I was nine;
but I thought that, lurking in the dark, there might
be spiders, so I dared not make those riches mine.

Granted, I survived my childhood frights
of spiders, failure, dark–and other bogeymen–
but how I let the dread of what *might* be
suck the juices from what may have been!

SMALL TOWN

Trouble is, I'm a transplant.
Had I always been in this pot,
in this corner of the garden,
with its precise two hours
of direct morning light
and dappled afternoon shade,
I might not know that I can bear
the furnace glare
of the desert's July sun.

They spin me one quarter turn
at regular intervals,
as if a symmetry of form
were my ideal as well as theirs.
Meanwhile, my roots
coil against terracotta walls in
repeated, frenzied circles
searching
for a way out.

Here, I am dwarfed and bound.
But when that day comes
for a larger container,
or for none at all. . .
on that day when
pruning is no more. . .
on that day
of reckoning. . .
I will soar.

Sometimes Bliss Begins as a Bitter Fruit

An olive, fresh from the tree,
is an offense to the tongue.
Who first imagined the harsh,
green oval could transmute, given
half a year with lye or salt and vinegar?

On this day in October,
(the month for harvesting green olives)
alone in a silent house,
I wait for the epiphany
I feel and fear is coming.

Then I recall the unopened jar
of antipasto olives
I have denied myself so far,
abundance waiting for permission
or a special occasion.

Two (all I need as manifesto)
green globes collapse between my teeth,
and I lick unfettered fingers clean
of aromatics, oil, and wine
married in the spicy marinade.

Not for the timid
is the search for joy.
Epiphany can be breaking the seal,
chancing dismay
for what it may reveal.

SHALL WE, LIKE SALOME . . .

Deciduous trees that have mastered deception
and flashed leaves of emerald the whole summer through
in fall, drop their guise of constant perfection,
revealing the hidden with each autumn hue.

Pigment and light emerge with the frost,
as each layer shimmers in unveiling dance,
shading through green, gold, crimson, and rust,
showing true colors, forsaking pretense.

We, too, wear the mask that so often deceives,
blindfold ourselves, and ignore the real prize.
Can we learn of our souls from the turning of leaves
by stripping delusion from unseeing eyes?

Knowing what's true in life's forest montage
takes finding the you beneath self-camouflage.

GIPSYING-PARTY

(gipsying-party: A party who meet to frolic in the open air.
–John Ogilvie, Comprehensive English Dictionary, 1865)

Oh! To dance in the open air,
to be tipsy in old Tipperary!
To be fancy free, let the gypsy in me
frolic and frisk and make merry!

But by walls I'm confined
and convention constrained,
by society's rules I'm abiding.
Yet, I'm loose in my mind;
in my heart, I'm unreined,
and my spirit is on a horse–Riding!

Is it enough to be free just in dreams,
or must those dreams walk abroad
to be as real to the soul as they seem,
when it seems they have come straight from God?

ODE TO SPRING

I sing no songs of yearning for an eternal Spring,
I am a desert dweller, and I know the vernal wind,
its growling voice, its gritty tongue, and its scouring blast.
My crisis years of chrysalis are safely in the past.

In seedling days of formless need, by instinct we survive.
Too young for noble purpose, we thrust toward light and thrive
in blind response to summons. We hear the horn of God,
which calls us through raw grains of sand, tangled roots, and sod.

It's only from the summer or beyond that we're aware
of life's full cyclic turnings. Memory must be there
as midwife to our concepts of renewal and rebirth.
For embryos in struggle, Spring is primeval First.

When I first ventured forth to learn how life and growth were done,
and spread frail, timid tendrils in the pale, returning sun,
cold winter crept back silently, and with deceitful frost,
withered one bold, shining shoot. I still recall its loss.

But if a wounded seedling can pass that first fierce test,
it learns the ancient wisdoms, tides of growth and rest.
Stronger still grow summer roots that know the springtime quake;
they plunge straight for bedrock when soul-sap comes awake.

I bask in harvest sunlight now, in burnished, golden rays
of mellow autumn fullness, September's sapphire haze.
I bloom, a strong chrysanthemum, on many sturdy stems
and bursts of countless petals unfolding from within.

I would not trade these amber days of rich autumnal worth
to run anew Spring's frantic race of pain and hurt and birth.
Because I know my childhood test is why I now stand tall,
I say the truest ode to Spring is what blooms in the Fall.

JUDGING BY HER WORDS

In Whose Name

I know you mean well, but
when I walk through my black night,
do not urge me to *have faith*.

Faith is not a commodity to be had,
nor a certainty I carry in my pocket.
To be found lacking in it
when I battle fear and doubt
is yet another burden.

When I am trying
to keep myself–or
a loved one–alive,
do not, I beg you,
ask me also to
keep the faith.

That onus is on you, or others,
while I am fighting demons.

Rather, reassure me that,
in some unbesieged cloister,
candlelit hands fold in prayer
and *keep the faith* on my behalf.

As I search for talisman
against catastrophe, despair,
do not dangle that word, *faith*,
just beyond my grasp,
lest I recall

the tiger crouched outside the door,
waiting with gleaming fang
for the moment that I falter.

To be truly kind, tell me that,
although I cannot retrieve my past
credentials of unshaken belief,
Faith has not forsaken me,
still calls me her *beloved child.*

The naming may be enough.

COSMIC SHIFT

Today a stranger said, "You are a star,"
and all my world then transformed, incandescent,
though it was, perhaps, a metaphor.

In its utterance, I was flung to a nebula afar,
spun in spiral orbit, made transcendent
by a word, when a stranger said, "You are." A star,

a twinkling, might hope that time would never bar
its chance to light a world where life lay nascent.
Perhaps it was a metaphor

that flashed across the Mind that governs Heaven, jarred
an inkling into action, made creative urges effervescent.
Do you wonder if it was a metaphor

that first set galaxies and life ablaze? Did God say, "You are . . .
. . . a Word" to transform the universe from its quiescence?
Today a stranger said, "You are a star,"
Though it was, perhaps, a metaphor.

HARVEST

Words spike from our souls as plants shoot from the earth.
Joy sings from our hills in drifts of daffodils,
yellow-throated choruses of life and birth.
Compassion is an aria of grass, green blades spill

and blend in emerald arpeggios and hymns.
Tones of inspiration rise like slender lodge pole pines.
Love spoken is a cedar, fragrant boughs that bend
but shelter still from fierce Sirocco winds.

But from our bogs and swamps, inaudible and dark,
germinate the words we should not speak.
Greed and pride sprout tongues piercing as bamboo.
Envy creeps in ivied whispers; blame bleeds its slow fatigue.

Prejudice and scorn writhe like thorn from clod.
Let us forbid the shade where they entwine.
Grant that we are wary of those usurpers, God,
and keep them in day's glare, their growth confined.

From memory's sweeping lawn,
let us uproot guilt and shame,
those bindweeds that, allowed to run,
choke away the sunlight, drink the rain.

Let us test the soils of our souls for truth
and see what seeds lie hidden in the loam,
what will blossom fair with water, light, and air,
what is dormant that, of itself, may bloom,

Before we set our sentences like scythes
to the harvest of our hearts and minds,
before we bundle grain with phrase or cord,
before we cast pronouncements on the winds

that blow toward the laborers who wait,
let us consider what our crop will yield
when it is flailed by threshers in the field,
when winnowed by the gleaner at the gate.

Pantomime in Porcelain

For days, loquacious Lulu had spoken not a word;
a case of laryngitis guaranteed she'd not be heard.
Pantomime was all she had to make her wishes known.
Into a fair Marcel Marceau this silenced girl had grown.

She stepped into a Ladies' Room (quite empty stood each stall),
settled in most comfortably–then heard disaster's call.
Basso profundo was the voice that from the doorway boomed,
"If anyone's in here, speak up! I've come to mop the room."

"Now what's a girl to do?" I ask. The motions that she made
(while eloquent and meaningful to her) were just charade.
How could she answer, or make known the fact that she was there?
She racked her brain, and then a plan was born of her despair.

Mutely mumbling cusswords that would make a sailor blush,
She put her trust in plumbing, which she flushed–
                                        and flushed–
                                                and flushed–

FLETCHERIZE

(fletcherize: To chew thoroughly. Derived from Horace Fletcher,
American diet and digestive health messiah, who advised chewing food
until all flavor was gone.)
–Mitford Mathew, *Dictionary of Americanisms*, 1956

Whether chewing on meat or chewing on words,
by experts we're often advised
to measure our movements, avoid the absurd;
in short, we must all fletcherize.

In swallowing words, I'll admit, I have erred,
and sometimes I said things unwise;
but, if no great debater, I'm a fair masticator
and, at least, my jaws get exercise.

If Webster Had Been a Poet

Shade cast by beach umbrellas
shelters from the sweltering sun,
bans the solar rays from overtanning
all those bathers in their shades.
Their Solar Rays and Raybans help them play
at looking cool in pool or on sun-dazzled sand.

Shades worn by day protect eyes looking out,
at night, protect from others looking in.
By some, they're worn for spectacles,
the quintessential accessory
for hip musician, cool Beat poet, hot celebrity,
a feigned disguise that instantly identifies.

Shades that cover windows—window blinds—
shield us from the blinding light of day;
but, we are more inclined to lower shades
to hide our secrets from the public's prying eyes.
Still, within, a little light casts shadows in parade;
thus, silhouettes confess in pantomime.

Those who live in deepest shade, the blind,
who do not need to shield their eyes
from glare, nonetheless wear shades.
Dare we ask why? In their mind's eye,
do shades deflect our pity, let them blend,
or shield them from the unrepentant stare?

Did black and blind Ray Charles don his shades
as a badge of his affliction, to be kind,

to salve the anguish of the sighted without insight
who could not bear to gaze into the ruins
and confront the hollow windows of the soul man
or see beyond the blinds of twice-deep shade?

Shades inhabit poems. Half-glimpsed spirits,
clothed in memory and nuance, haunt the dreams
of poet dreamers, who strive to apprehend
the influence of these shrouded shades of meaning
who float like specters of illusion or expression,
waiting 'til the poet finds the words for resurrection.

Shades walk unshackled in the worlds of art;
shallow lines, with shading, gain perspective.
Shades of purple glide across the spectrum, mauve
to *aubergine* (humble eggplant given *nom de guerre*
to fight in fashion's fall-to-winter runway wars).
Alas, poor orchid, draped in mourning hues!

Among the Nightshades, Aubergine stands innocent;
not so, her toxic cousin, Belladonna–
Deadly Nightshade or *Fair Lady* are her other names–
but she is dark, not fair, this blossom of wide,
brilliant eyes and berries that, against bruise-purple leaves,
startle–just before they fade to black.

Hearts first race for Belladonna, then they faint
and falter, pursuing the phantasm of dreams.
They drown in her nectar at *L'Auberge de Mort*,
lodging place for travelers through Hades.
Belladonna, deadly siren of the night,
lures the lonely, brokenhearted
down, down, down. . .
to be Shades.

Better Left Unsaid

What mad god

set the blue nebula of speech spinning,
loosed garrulous galaxies

to fling
      Word Stars

through the white hole
        of my throat?

    I try to call them back, but
not one–   not one.

They chatter down the lattices of space.

        spiral galaxies
        arms outflung in ecstasy
        spin like dervishes

POCKET POEM

Poetry is
the gift of song upon a pair of lips once mute
a touch of light on eyes perversely blind
compassion in the heart of uncouth brute
a new idea in a rigid mind
a way to carry wonder in a pocket
a way to wash away the wounds of time
a way to banish anger, or to lock it
where it cannot do much hurt–in rhyme.

Noncommittal

Having been told that she was the prize
only to learn he had others as well,

> Having tasted her honey-tongued lies
> only to find she was his Jezebel,

Knowing the pain caused
by giving her heart,

> Knowing she'd left, but not
> what made them part,

their encounter could have become a romance,
but both had been burned and would not take the chance.

The participles of risk kept them dangling.
The past imperfect of love left them
hanging.

Exercising Discretion

In the gathering before T'ai Chi class,
as shoes come off and purses
are stashed out of the way . . .
as the minute hand
ticks toward the twelve . . .
in that time before convocation . . .

the widows, divorcees, disappointed ones
speak their cynicism,
enumerate the betrayals.

The long-married housewife bewails
her husband's impending retirement,
as if complaining
about more time together
were the fashionable
and socially correct thing to do.

I keep silent, wife of four decades,
grateful
for his trust, which freed me to fly,
his urging to follow my passion,
the fidelity of our partnership.

I remember, too,
the aching months apart,
heeding calls of war and duty.
When will his retirement come?
How do you reclaim lost years?

Among these bitter women,
requited love seems heresy.
Three of us say nothing.
The others would not believe us,
and it doesn't do to boast.

Why I Don't Write You Love Sonnets

You have more than earned
a paltry fourteen lines.
Neither Bard nor Portuguese
had more cause than I
to inscribe a lover's name with immortality.

God knows I've tried.
Sometimes the words seem nearly right,
epiphany hovers, then flits away.
A cadence almost captures what I want to say.
I reach for my pen, but then

flashback to my fifteenth summer, when
I netted butterflies, bees, and more—
scores of the glittering and gauzy-winged
who thickened August air at Hansons' farm.

Oh, I was the diligent student,
harvesting the harvesters at peak:
fatal jar, formaldehyde, insects preserved
(laid by for winter's course in Life Sciences).

Careful not to tatter wings with too much handling,
I speared thorax after thorax
with stainless quilting pins,
wedding tiny brides to sterile Styrofoam
under neatly scripted labels
Latinate, clinical, dispassionate.

When I wrote in names I knew them by:

Swallowtail, Sphinx, Honeybee,
June Bug, Mud Dauber,
my pen reeked of murder.

If I should try to net the fleeting moments
that have brought us to constancy,
the ephemeral flights we've taken
in the steady flow of each other,
the minute shifts to make a space
where both might sip
from lavender and clover–

surely, smudges would darken
my static fingertips,
as accusing as
moth dust.

Low-tide Catechism

The hour for nature's confessional is low tide,
in which all is revealed, from barnacled docks
to oyster beds left desolate by the sea's retreat.
When waters ebb, secrets yield, as if a shield had dropped
between priest and penitent, with no room to hide.

In this pulse, shore birds with blurring scissors' stride
and eyes like sharp, black beads swarm the flats; perform
an inquisition of the shallows; their greedy beaks
roll shells aside, probe gravel shifted by the tide
in search of small, reluctant martyrs fleeing, hidden.

Crustaceans burrow in contrition, pretend
to disappear, like secrets cloistered in the mind.
Do they hear the slide of shifting grains with dread,
fear the scarlet chamber, which seines the drifting sands
set tumbling by the piper's hungry tread?

The burnished stems of wetlands rushes,
blessed by the holy waters' inland flow
and touched by slanting sunlight, come aglow,
as if a master's hand were wielding them, like brushes,
painting domes of air in tints of Michelangelo.

When tides recede, the marshes wear a coat of mud;
reeds fade, as if the artist branded his meek tools
heretics and abandoned them, arrayed upon a rack.
Then, they put on sackcloth hues, stand in dull,
mute rows, like monks exploring silence to find God.

But why should I presume that low tide has revealed
a world where the ordained is reason to repent?
Although I recoil, nature seems at ease in *dishabille*;
untidiness provokes no shame, seems no less Heaven sent
than flood. Rising, falling–an equal sacrament.

Afterword

by
Marjorie Rommel, cofounder and program director
since the mid-1960s of The Northwest Renaissance,
a coalition of poets, performers, and publishers

Holocaust survivor and logotherapy founder Viktor Frankl (1905-1997) speaks of the *will* to meaning as necessary bravery, a moral imperative that transcends its origin in the German camps to impose on our thinking the *fact* of our responsibility, not only for our thoughts and actions, but to *make sense* of our circumstances—even the most sordid, bleak, painful, or despairing—to find in them reason to continue living "in spite of everything," and in living to discover some indestructible personal joy.

Toward these discoveries, Frankl works as intricately within the circles of humanist psychology and Jewish Law as Tesla did within the coils of his fantastic, futuristic, often hair-raising contrivances.

Shirley Balance Blackwell works within a far wider range: the continually transformative dimensions of human thought and poetic form. Otherwise, we would not—could not—have this volume of fiercely intelligent, intensely inquiring poems that examine the universe we only *think* we know, carefully observing its apparent phenomena, their shapes and dimensions and their possible meanings, both in themselves and for us.

For Blackwell, form provides a framework, and within it, freedom to explore the tangled limits of language and thought. Her rhymes are as much rhymes of music and meaning as of word usage; they peel back the layers of language to reveal intriguing and potentially troubling possibilities of physical fact at its intersection with human thought and emotion. In Shirley's hands, from this knotty intersection bursts an unexpected, truly indestructible, personal joy.

It has been my very great pleasure to know and work with Shirley, to watch the intricate turns of her mind, attention, and spirit, the increasing depth and range of her work. It's also my personal delight to have a pretty good idea what's coming next—and to know you're going to love it!

Stay tuned. Shirley Blackwell is definitely a poet to keep your eye on!

—Marjorie Rommel, Auburn, Washington, October 2011

ABOUT THE AUTHOR

Shirley Balance Blackwell grew up in the desert southwest. She married young, moved to Florida for three years, Colorado for a decade, and then to the nation's capital. There, she had a career as editor and analyst in an agency supporting top national security policymakers; she earned several awards for her job-related writing. Sideline poetic tributes to colleagues and send-ups of office routines may also have earned her the title of America's most prolific author of classified poetry. She has won numerous honors and prizes in national poetry contests.

Upon retiring from federal service, Blackwell returned to her home state of New Mexico and the creative and public writing she longed to do. She was a newspaper poetry columnist during 2006-09. She became president of the New Mexico State Poetry Society in 2011, after holding the post of 2010 New Mexico Senior Poet Laureate. She lives 20 miles south of Albuquerque with her husband, Louis, and two large rescue dogs, a black Labrador and a brown Vizsla (best guess).

www.ingramcontent.com/pod-product-compliance
Lightning Source LLC
Chambersburg PA
CBHW030933090426
42737CB00007B/412